Daisies and Moonlight

AF632824

Gracelyn Troxell

BookLeaf Publishing

Presentation by *BookLeaf Publishing*

Web: www.bookleafpub.com

E-mail: info@bookleafpub.com

ISBN: 9789357210041

First edition 2022

DEDICATION

To my friends, who will be forced to read this book.

ACKNOWLEDGEMENT

I would like to thank, my creative writing teachers, thank you for helping me discover writing and coaching me along the way.
Aurora, who has read many rough drafts of my poems and listened to many of my tangents.
Mr. Prev, for giving me the skills I need to write.
My friends and family who have helped get me to where I am.

Calling

Go and write.
What?
The story that you are too scared to tell.
The story that you feel you can never share.
The story that you will be judged for.
The story that others may need.

Guide to Understanding Poetry

How can one look at a poem,
and determine its worth?
How can one look at art,
and see it as merely paint on a canvas?
How can one look at a soul,
strewn across blankness and think you
understand it?
How can one simply look at a poem,
and understand it?

Destined

Brave.

Ha.
If only you really knew.
The thought put into every action I do.
I wouldn't be considered brave if they saw me rehearse in the mirror

Self-Assured.

Anything but.
I have to read affirmations in the morning to even pretend that I like myself.
I have to change my outfit too many times to count.
Not because I have to look perfect.
But because I need to at least feel okay in my own skin before leaving the house.

Honest

In my head.
Never out loud.

How it Started

It started with ballet shoes and tutus.
Hairspray, lipstick and blush.
Rushed costume changes.
Hot, pounding stage lights.

Then it was choir risers and pretty dresses.
Singing, speaking parts, acting.
Stressed music teachers.
Gymnasium filled with parents.

Next was music stands and sheet music.
Stress, note reading, counting.
Fiddle music.
Playing for people.

Then it was fields and memorizing music.
Marching, freezing, late nights.
Stadium Lights.
Bleachers full of people.

Now, it is love.
learning, performing, practicing.
Nerves.
Amazing.

Notes From the Soul

One of the earliest forms of music was spoken
word poetry.
The beat of the heart.
And notes from the soul.

The epic poem.
About an absolute nobody.
Goes Down In history.

The beat of the heart
The notes of the soul
Singing for others to listen.

Just maybe someone will listen.
To the beat.
To the notes.

Coffee Shops

Walking into the warmth,
Welcoming smiles,
Paintings and mismatched chairs,
Mismatched cups and chattering,
Live music and open mic nights,
The epitome of self-expression.
Chalk menu boards,
Hard-wood floors,
The best conversations.

The Worst Kind of Trapped

Forced into submission,
A silent type of quiet anger,
Reserved looks,
Quivering hands,
Settling into compliance,
Without any other options,
Without support,
He worst kind of trapped.

Home Away from Home

Comforting warmth,
And constant noise.
Scattered conversations,
And the sound of an espresso machine.
Leaning against a wall to access the outlets.
Scattered hair ties from long practices,
And phones buzzing on the stands.
Home away from home.

"You don't know me."

Passionate
Burnt out
Hard working
Scared of letting someone down
Procrastinator
Depressed
Punctual
Anxious

"Someday you will see..."

The truth.
How amazing you are.
That you deserve everything.
That if they do not like you, they are not worth it.
What we see.
What the world sees.
That your opinion of yourself is wrong.

Unlikely Friends

I never thought that this would work.
I am not the type to open up.
To be vulnerable.
To be able to rely on people around me.
To be willing to put my life on the line for them.
To get over old opinions.
Unlikely but not Impossible.

One. Last. Song.

Light filtered in through the multitude of tree branches. The smell of pine and freshly rained on dirt fills my nose as I wander further amongst the pine trees.
There it was again, resonating through the trees.
A piano.
Singing with agony, the pain of something long lost.
A lone wolf.
A dying flower.
An encaged bird.
A single thread, simplistic.
How was it that the gentle coaxing of a melodious piece could hold as much depth as the oceans can hold water?
Each step brought a wave, crashing over you, trapping you, like a needle and thread weaving between the trees, sewing me into different harmonies and dynamics.
Howling.
Wilting.
Crying.
It is like a sirens call. Pulling me towards the depths of the moving themes and what they hold.

The forest acting like a concert hall, echoing
back pebbles oh sadness, and longing.
Why is there a piano out here?
And what prompted such agony?
Like an earthquake, vibrating all around me.
Then all the trees, opening like curtains on a
stage. Illuminated by an extra celestial glow.
A piano,
The piano.
There at the edge of the clearing I stopped.
Perched on the edge of a black leather clad piano
bench sat, what appeared to be a man.
Light refracting through the mist he seemed to
be composed of.
Then like scissors cutting thread, the song cut
off.
A wall of silence.
Then like a waterfall, an ocean fell upon the
keys of coal and chalk.
An odd sight to behold, a translucent man,
weeping at a piano.
The salty drops, after time stopped plinking
down.
The figure looks at me,
Images,
Of standing ovations,
Dances with women in silk gowns,
Symphonies moving with each other like an
ocean's waves,

The shutting of a pianos lid,
A private jet,
A news story.
The figure motions for me to approach the piano.
As I draw closer, what would be his hands delicately hover over the keys,
Then a lone bird whistling its heart into an empty forest,
The warmth of the sun,
A sculpture of light and water.
As he painted in the air, his hands slowly took on shape. Clearly well practiced, his hand flitted over the keys.
Slowly crawling up from his fingertips color and a solidity.
In a mourner's uniform, he sat there.
A picture of mountains,
Souring angels
Then silence.
Eyes meet.
A smile.
Then nothing.

A Dream

Green fields.
Hair floating with the wind.
A mighty castle in the backdrop.
Laughing.
Running.
The sound of water running.
Twirling.
Weaving.
Choreography.
Warm arms.
The sun shining down.
The grass between my toes.
Falling back into the grass.

A "All About Me" Poem

The color green,
But not the ugly manufactured green,
The green hues from the trees, plants, and
piercing eyes.

Essential Oils,
For headaches and congestion.
Sometimes just because I like to smell like
orange and sandalwood.

Stained hands,
From dragging my hand through the words I just
wrote,
Paint and charcoal stains.

Hand-written letters,
because sometimes writing is easier then
speaking,
because I always want to communicate in a way
that best expresses what I feel.

Crystals,
Not because I necessarily believe in their power,
But because they won't hurt, and I need all the
help I can get.

Poems,
So that I can express myself,
In a way that makes sense to me.

Lament

When it rains it pours,
Or at least thats how the story goes.
Running will get you no where,
But the bravery to stay is rare.
Facing every day with dread,
but there is nothing to do instead.
So all we can do is sit and repent,
and hope God hears this lament.

Childhood

The smell of rain as I jumped in the gutter
The smell of books in the office
Scraped knees
Home-cooked meals
The smell of autumn leaves
Watching Food Network
The ugly pink porcelain of the bathroom
The guitars in the basement
The fancy doghouse that my dad built
Scrapbooking supplies
Playgrounds
Memories

Ashes

Spread to thin,
doing too much.
Then again,
who can really tell when enough is enough?

Slowly burning myself out,
till there is nothing left to give.
You can't hear me shout,
just trying to live.

Fatal

I always place myself in these positions,
Nobody's fault but my own,
Allowing myself to be lulled into a false sense of security.

It All Takes Time

You cannot rush confrontation
You cannot stare at yourself in the mirror,
And take the deepest parts of yourself
To be put on display for others.

It is not as easy as just looking.
It is like looking through a lens,
Clouded with years of hurt,
Hiding,
Loathing.

You cannot rush confrontation
You cannot stare at yourself in the mirror,
And take the deepest parts of yourself
To be put on display for others.

You can only repeat yourself.
Hoping the people trying to get a glimpse,
Will understand.
The pain.
Hatred.
Hiding.

You cannot rush confrontation
You cannot stare at yourself in the mirror,

And take the deepest parts of yourself
To be put on display for others.

My Inspiration

A sky full of stars,
long rehearsals,
the smell of freshly brewed coffee,
long nights,
early days,
library study nights,
jam sessions,
campfires,
people.

Daisies and Moonlight

Twirling in the starlight,
Barefoot in the grass,
Distant strumming guitar,
Singing and dancing and laughter,

Blooming innocence,
Bathed in the light,
Despite the darkness
Just enough to reflect everything around it,

Stargazing,
Warm tea and stained fingers,
Observations and dreams,
Daisies and Moonlight.

www.ingramcontent.com/pod-product-compliance
Lightning Source LLC
Chambersburg PA
CBHW051756130826
49812CB00033B/1178